Northern Nib

# The Scent of Romance

## and other Barmy Ballads from Ireland!

### Poetry by Robert E. Wilson
### Illustrations by Aisling Wilson

# Contents

# Introduction

When a friend who'd enjoyed my first two books said, 'I've got a new challenge for you,' I couldn't resist the temptation! He then proceeded to ask me if, in my next book, I'd tackle a question that was undoubtedly close to his heart: *'How does a pig farmer find romance?'*

Well, as you can see, I rose to this literary challenge and have given the subject pride of place in this, my third collection of barmy ballads with a distinctively Irish flavour!

As always, I try to show that poetry can be about anything that inspires you and can be read and enjoyed by everyone. As with the pieces in my earlier books, some of the ballads here will lend themselves to public performance reading (and have been thoroughly tested on the longsuffering members of my writers' group).

The tales relayed in this volume are set in all four provinces of Ireland, so don't be too quick to laugh at folk in one neck of the woods before you've read the ballads about yours!

Once again, I have to say a sincere word of thanks to author and poet Lynda Tavakoli, who so faithfully tutors and encourages our writers' group. Thanks also to all my fellow writers for their appreciation and feedback and, of course, an enormous word of thanks to my daughter Aisling for her original and excellent illustrations.

**Robert E. Wilson, October 2017.**

## About the Author and Artist:

**Robert E. Wilson** is from County Antrim, Northern Ireland. An active member of an established writers' group, he contributed to the 'Linen Poetry and Prose Anthology' published in partnership with the Irish Linen Centre, Lisburn, which is available on Kindle. He is a reader at the 'Purely Poetry' evenings in the Crescent Arts Centre, Belfast, has participated in the Bard of Armagh Festival of Humorous Verse and was a finalist in the Connemara Mussel Festival Poetry Competition 2016, judged by the esteemed Irish poet Eamon Grennan.

Along with this collection, Robert's first two books of humorous poems are available on Amazon.

For further information on Robert's work, visit his website: www.northernnib.weebly.com or follow on Twitter @WilsonNib

**Aisling Wilson** is an artist currently based in Northern Ireland, having graduated with a First Class Honours Degree in Fine Art from Ulster University and studied abroad for a year at Waynesburg University, Pennsylvania, USA.

For further information on Aisling's work, visit her website: www.aislingwilson.co.uk or follow on instagram @aislingwilson artist

# The Scent of Romance

## *a pig farmer's tale...*

*If you've read 'Like Your New View, Hugh?' in my second book, 'A Bit of Skullduggery...' there's mention of a pig farmer named Fred. Well, this ballad is the story of Fred's rather exasperating search for the ideal date, spurred on by his friend, the well-meaning but hapless Dave McTeer from my first book, 'The Cullybackey Counterfeiters...'*

My name's Fred McCaughey,

I'm tall and I'm gawky,

I know, but I scrub up not bad;

I'm a hard-workin' fella,

Son of Billy and Ella –

Ach, everyone liked me oul dad!


His farm was well-known –

Good products, home-grown,

But now, it's just me by myself;

Sure, I still run the place,

But today it's a case

Of what's best to put on the shelf..


Like the meat we produce.

Ach, there's no blinkin' use

In pretendin' that times haven't changed;

Sure, the need for choice grew

And the subsidies, too –

I got the whole farm rearranged..

To suit new demands –

It meant hiring more hands,

And those departmental bigwigs

Laid down rules to follow;

Though it's hard to swallow,

The thing I got into is *pigs!*


Well, that leads me to this –

There's no wedded bliss

For a fella in my line of farmin';

Where you'll make a fair bob,

Just remember, this job

Your chance of romance will be harmin'!


Now, they say, 'Where there's muck,

There is brass,' so, with luck,

I *should* be a 'good catch', think you?

I'm a bachelor boy,

The well-healed real McCoy,

And a young lad of just forty-two!

Then, why am I single?

As if I don't mingle

With girls in the Young Farmers Clubs;

I've the gift o' the gab,

So why can't I nab

A woman in one of the pubs?


Well, I'm sure you've guessed why –

Whenever I try

To get a nice date, if they sniff

The slightest wee hint

Of my job, off they'll sprint

Like lemmings clean over a cliff!


Ach, I use every trick –

The deodorant stick

And aftershave, but once she learns

What I do for a livin'

She'll have some misgivin' –

The mood of the evenin' just turns!

Well, my mate, Kevin Rice

Tried to be awful nice

And play down the problem for me –

'Is it worth contemplatin'

Some internet datin'?

Ach, Fred – why not try it and see?'


So, I started to footer

About the computer

And came to a wee site or two

That said: *'Forty-Plus?*

*Come and sign up with us –*

*We'll help find the right match for you!'*


Then, one night while up late,

I landed a date

With a lassie from out near Buckna,

So I pressed my dark suit

And I tried hard to put

Best foot forward, to quote me dear ma!

Well, I felt at first glance

The scent of romance!

(Maybe that's the wrong word to use here!)

We'd arranged to have dinner –

Was I on to a winner?

The picture would soon become clear!


Things looked promising, though,

With her glass of Bordeaux

She stood at the bar. Then I spoke:

'Let's sit at this trough –

I mean *table!* Some broth

Would be nice, then a salmon that's smoked!'


(When we sat down to dine

With a glass of fine wine,

Would she look for the source of a *smell?*

Then, wait 'till you see –

She'll trace it to me!

In no time at all could she tell?)

Then my date, name of Valerie,

Said, 'I have a gallery

Along the main street in Broughshane.

'What's your job? – I make sculpture.'

I replied, 'Agriculture –

I've a wee farm that's out near the Maine.'


Well, when she heard *that*,

It changed our whole chat –

Her relatives, Carol and Hugh

Lived there, but its charm

A neighbouring farm

Had destroyed when some *pigs* arrived – *phew!*


Right! I knew that was it –

'Twas the time now to quit;

The farm that she'd mentioned was mine!

I reckoned she'd guessed

And was not too impressed

At dating a bloke who farms swine!

That's what happened each time,

Like it was a crime

To open a pig farm today!

Ach, this sounds like a huff,

But I said, 'That's enough

Of this nonsense – I'm up and away..


To cast my net wide!

I've tried and I've *tried!*

Yon herd o' pigs scares them away;

I should book a wee break,

Ach, I might even take

A couple o' months or so, hey!'


So, I put my farm's land

In to the safe hand

Of a manager, Ricky McKnight,

And said, 'Keep it runnin',

I'm goin' to London,

As soon as I get me a flight!'

My oul mate, Dave McTeer,

Who used to live here

In a wee farm that's up near Buckna,

Said, 'My flat's there – no joke –

(Well, it's really dad's folk,

My Uncle Ed and Auntie Fra..

Who own it). They say,

"Let your friends come and stay,"

And London's the place *you* should be

If you're stuck for romance

And want a good chance

Of datin' somewhere that's pig-free!'

Well, I'd need a wee job

To earn a few bob

And pay for my lodgings – and *date* –

So, I said, 'Dave, look out,

And give me a shout

If *you* see a *job* for me, mate!'

I was there just four days

When Dave comes and says,

'I've got some great news for ye, Fred –

I know it's short warnin' –

There's a job in the mornin'

With a mate of my oul Uncle Ed!


I'm no' sure what it is,

But it's soundin' like his

Mate's in retail. Here's where you're to go:

Aspen Way, close to here;

Hey, Canary Wharf's near –

Sounds the old business district, you know!


*And,* I've found you a *date* –

She's a friend of my mate

Kenny Mulligan, called Maggie Spence;

She works in *'Elite'*,

A top London boutique,

And I hear that she likes country gents!

If some dosh you can clink,

She'll probably think

You've got a top job in the City;

Likes her blokes well-coiffured

And she might be allured

If she thinks you've got cash in the kitty!


I've been able to fix

You a meal – it's at six,

In a restaurant called "Junction One";

But you'll have to go straight

From your work to the date,

So, dress nice and smart, me oul son!'


Well, next morning, I rose,

And donned my best clothes,

And boarded the bus, fresh and bright;

My confidence great

'Bout this job and my date –

No trace of a pig farm tonight!

*Well,* when I got back

To the flat, 'What's the craic?

You're home early,' Dave curiously said.

I replied, 'Just don't ask!'

Then he grinned, 'Z'at a mask?

You've a face like an oul Lurgan spade!'


'I left lookin' smart,'

I spluttered, 'to start

In an office job – or so I thought;

D'ye want to know, mate,

Why Maggie, my date,

From beginnin' to end sat there fraught?


Just smell me now, can't ye?

*That's* some place ye sent me –

Take a whiff o' my hair and my clothes!

And, Dave, to be frank,

That restaurant stank –

Mags did everything but hold her nose..

For, that job - what a stench!

Standin' there at a bench

And carryin' crate after crate!

Boy, I smelt appallin',

The job was a stall in –

*The fish market at Billingsgate!'*

# An Open-and-Shut Decision

## a 'rail' tale...

*It's straight down the line to see if this station master's on the right track when it comes to a bit of local logic!*

There's a quaint old railway station ten miles west of Castlebar,
Where the track runs left-to-right across the road;
It's a sleepy, rural crossing where you'll scarcely see a car
And the pace of life most certainly has slowed.

The station-master at this quiet spot is Gerry Byrne,
A wee man pushing seventy today;
Sweat wouldn't break upon his brow – ach, nothing of concern
Ever rattles or disturbs folk down that way.

Now, Russell P. Zokowski, from Cookeville, Tennessee
Came to Ireland, searching for his Irish roots;
He'd rented a convertible, was motoring carefree
Yet purposefully, down some scenic routes.

As Russ came near that crossing, he said, 'Somethin's kinda weird,'
So he stopped and briefly tooted on his horn;
Then, from the station, in no rush, old Gerry Byrne appeared –
Cap, jacket, boots and man a bit shopworn.

'Hey, buddy!' Russell cried. 'What's goin' on? I can't get through –
One gate here's closed, the other's open wide!'
'Sure, sir,' said Gerry, 'there is nothin' here to worry you –
I man these gates efficiently, with pride.

Would I be right to say now, sir, you're from the USA,
And would your name suggest some Irish genes?'
'It's actually *Zokowski*,' Russell said, 'and, by the way,
Although I'm not so sure of what it means..

My grandma was called *Murphy*; she was born outside Tralee
And her father came from Westport,' added Russ;
'So, that's why I've come all the way from Cookeville, Tennessee,
For my Irish ancestry I'd like to suss..

But, something's really puzzling me,' said Russ, with worried frown,
'Your railway track runs straight across this road;
One gate is opened up, I see, the other's firmly down –
I think some explanation now I'm owed!'

'Well, sir,' said Gerry, 'if you have a minute, I'll explain –
These gates have been placed here to keep you safe;
Without them, if you drove across the track, a comin' train
Might hit you – *CRASH!* – and it would more than chafe..

You, sir – you're dead!  So, that's why every single day,
When one's expected, I come out, I do
And close the gates sir, once it's gone, and you'll go on your way,
For I'll open them again, to let you through!

Now, sir, you must agree I'd not be lookin' after you
If you headed, in your nifty new sports car
Across the line when some big busy train is hurtlin' through
And carried you the length of Castlebar!'

'So, buddy, let me get this straight,' mused Russ, a bit perplexed;
'You're saying that, so everyone's protected,
These gates are open when no train is coming down the tracks,
But you close both, as soon as one's expected?'

'You're on to it!' Said Gerry. Still, Russ puzzled in his head.

'Tell me,' he said, 'and I'll be on my way –

Why is there only *one* gate open?' – Gerry winked and said,

'Sure, I'm only *half-expectin'* one today!'

# Transatlantic Toast

## *a tale of absent friends...*

*A*s I'm sure you'll gather from a few of these ballads, we have our own form of logic in Ireland (and, contrary to widespread opinion, it does make perfect sense)! Here's another example of how it works...

Three mates from Letterkenny, called Eamon, Mike and Pat
Met every Friday night in Grogan's Bar for drinks and chat;
They never failed to make it there, come rain, hail, frost or snow,
And sat 'till old Frank Grogan told them it was time to go.

They shared the same old stories, they cracked the same old jokes,
Three easy-going lads who came from good old country folks;
They sat for hours and blethered till they finished their last stout,
Then poor old Frank, he had a job to get those three lads out!

But then one evening, Eamon said, 'Now, I don't want to ruin
The craic tonight, but I should say what Ann an' me are doin'..
I'm told that, in the plumbin' trade, there's lots of work today
For lads with skills like mine if I go to the USA..

So, we're leavin' here next month and headin' off to New York City;
I know I'll miss you eejits, and that's just an awful pity.
I should have told you sooner, but to do that I declined
For, knowin' you lads, you'd both try to make me change my mind!'

Well, Eamon's mates went quiet for the first time in their lives –
You could've cut the silence round their table with blunt knives;
Eventually, Mike gulped, then spoke, 'But we've been comin' here
On Fridays since the year o' dot for banter, buzz and beer!'

Now, to be honest, things just weren't the same from that night on –
The fellows knew, deep in their hearts, the craic had somehow gone;
Then on Eamon's final evening, as they sat in Grogan's Bar,
Mike said, 'Hey, mate, we all know that New York is right an' far..

But we *also* know it's comin' down wi' loads of Irish bars,
So you should have no trouble findin' one to have some jars;
Just promise us you'll drink three pints each Friday – always *three* –
One for yourself and one for Pat and then a pint for me!'

'That way, we'll keep our bond alive,' said Pat, 'till you come back.'
'But, if you never do,' smiled Mike, 'you'll always mind the craic!'
'You have my word,' said Eamon, 'an' I'll never let you down –
I'll have three pints each Friday night, when I'm out on the town!'

The fateful day arrived and off went Eamon and wife Ann,

But, good lad, he did not forget his drinking partners' plan –

He frequented an Irish Bar not far from where he worked,

And always ordered three pints – his devotion never shirked!

Well, as the years passed, barman Eugene got to know him well,

And always had those three pints ready, calling it 'darn swell'

That Eamon drank a toast to his old mates in Donegal,

Sat in their pub as nights grew dark in what he called 'the fall'.

Then one Friday night in springtime, Eamon ordered only two,

Instead of three, pints as it was his normal thing to do;

He did the same the next week, and then the next again –

He'd drink a first, then second pint but from a third abstain.

Well, by the fourth week, Eugene's curiosity was such,

He thought that, in a careful manner, he should really touch

On why our Eamon left one drink out – he should surely say,

So he addressed the matter in a friendly sort of way:

'Hey, Eamon, I don't want to pry, but recently I see

That you are only drinking *two* pints – it was always *three*

You ordered.  I hope things aren't rough; tell me, is work okay?

Are both your buddies still around, or has one passed away?'


'No, my job's fine,' smiled Eamon back, 'as far as I can tell,

And my two mates in Donegal are both alive and well,

An' I'm not keepin' tabs on all the money that I've spent –

This pint's for Mike, that one's for Pat – *I'm* off the drink for Lent!'

# The Mighty Mussel

## *a celebratory tale...*

I was delighted and privileged to be among seven 'Honourable Mentions' in an international poetry competition which formed part of the 2016 Connemara Mussel Festival in County Galway. This is the poem I wrote and had the pleasure of reading at the event.

At the risk now of startin' to blow,

The whole blinkin' lot of us know

When it comes to cuisine

That Ireland's supreme

And has to its credit a great gourmet scene.

But, surely it's time now to shout

'Bout a secret that's bound to get out;

Sure, from Clare to Fermanagh,

Tralee to Falcarragh,

The word's going round about – *psssst!* – Connemara!


You see, when it comes to a dish,

We Irish are fond of our fish;

Ach, you just can't go wrong

With the Dublin Bay prawn

And think of those lobster-pots pulled up at dawn;

And then there's our prized local salmon,

Caught fresh from the banks of the Shannon!

*But…* from Tullow to Tara,

And Cork to Cloondara –

There's talk of the fine *mussel* in Connemara!

Sure, you're thinkin' that mussels are small,

To catch them, you don't need to trawl,

Or cast out a line

When the forecast is fine,

But, hey! Just you try them with cream and white wine!

Now, some are prepared to go far

To sample the best caviar,

But they'll come from Alaska

And Guadalajara

To savour those mussels in old Connemara!


So, maybe you're missing a trick

If you don't get to Tullycross, quick!

There's a lot of elation –

In all of creation,

Has such a small shellfish seen such celebration?

Those humble wee mussels have – well,

Now really come out of their shell!

So, wheel your wheelbarra'

Through streets broad and narra'

As long as those mussels are from… Connemara!


*Then, let's take a break from the hustle and bustle,*

*And raise high our glasses to one mighty mussel!*

# A Bicycle Made for..
# *Who?*

## *a 'tyre-ing' tale...*

*This tale really is based on a true story, confirmed by relatives of both characters. These are the same fellows who featured in the 'Rocky Road to Dublin...' poem in my last book but, as always, the story is well-embellished!*

Two oul mates, Jack and Tommy, born and raised in Belfast town
Were sitting in the famous local bar that's called 'The Crown'
When Tommy said, 'I'm worried that we're puttin' on a bit;
D'ye not think we should have a go at tryin' to get fit?'

'Suppose ye'r right,' Jack pondered. 'Here's us sittin' drinkin' stout
When we should both be exercisin' – aimin' to get out
To do a bit o' walkin' or a bit o' runnin' too.'
'Hey, I've just thought,' smiled Tommy, 'of the very thing to do..

A fella in my work called Jim, who lives near Castlereagh
Tells me his wife and him go cyclin' nearly every day;
Ach, he's a guy who'd lend his bike to anyone at random –
That's anyone who's game enough to ride upon a *tandem!'*

'You mean a bike that's built for two?' said Jack, with puzzled frown.
'Exactly, mate,' laughed Tommy. 'Why don't me and you go roun'
And ask him if he'll let us use it in week or two,
When him and Anne go off to spend the weekend in Portnoo?

Look, Jack, if he's not usin' it, let's give this thing a try!
Who knows? If we both like it, we might even want to buy
One for ourselves! Think of the craic! I'm sure our wives won't mind;
Your Maisie would just love it – you in front and her behind!'


'All right,' said Jack, 'but, let me tell you, I'm not just as sure
As you are, Tommy and it isn't me just soundin' dour;
Ach, mate – you know me, I'm that wee bit harder to convince!'
'Look, Jack,' said Tommy, 'don't you worry – it'll all be sinch!'


Then, a couple of days later, Tommy came to Jack and said,
'Mate, Jim and Anne are headin' off *this* Friday, so instead
Of waitin' for a week or two, let's go! My nephew, Stan
Drives past Jim's every night – he'll bring the tandem in his van.'


And so, on Thursday evening, there they were, all set to go:
Jack said, 'Ach, you've convinced me. Do you mind my brother, Joe?
He's always boastin' that he rides his bike ten miles each day,
An' thinks we're getting' old and fat – I wonder what he'd say..

If we arrived at his front door some mornin' – me and you,

Lookin' neat upon-the-seat of a bike that's built for two?

Ach, still, he lives in Cushendun – a brave wee bit away;

Let's think of somewhere near to go this comin' Saturday!'


'I think we *should* head up the coast,' said Tommy. 'Cushendun

Is really not *that* far away; c'mon – it might be fun

To visit Joe and all!  My sister Kate, his better half

Will send us off well-fed!  Let's go – it's bound to be a laugh!'


'Hmm… still against my better judgment,' muttered Jack, 'but then

If we don't make good use of it, I 'spose we don't know when

We'll get to use the bike again. Ach, it'll be a quare

Oul geg to see the face o' Joe as soon as we get there!'


'Good man yer da!' said Tommy. 'Ach, I'm glad you're keen to go!'

'There's only one thing,' Jack replied, 'I think you'd better know:

I'm just a wee bit worried, mate, by what your drivin's like –

If you don't mind, old son, I'll take the front seat on the bike!'

So, on Saturday at half-past nine, the two of them rode off,

With trousers tucked well down their socks; each one felt like a toff

Aboard the tandem, Jack in front and Tommy at the rear –

Quite honestly, the cut o' them was something else...man dear!


They thought they'd head to Larne town, then cycle up the coast,

'And, if we're there by ten,' said Jack, 'let's stop for tea and toast

At some wee café, then hop on, and off we'll go again!

Revived and fresh, we'll soon be ridin' up toward the glen!'


But, as the bold Jack pedalled on, the strain began to show;

The speed at which they travelled soon became, well, rather slow.

They didn't get to Larne by ten, 'twas closer to eleven.

'That was wild,' puffed Jack, 'but there's a café here, thank heaven!'


They parked the tandem, went inside and Jack flopped on a seat,

While Tommy, on the other hand, still looked quite fresh and neat.

Jack ordered one strong mug of tea, whilst Tommy gave a sigh:

'I'm going to get stuck into a great big Ulster Fry!'

Jack still felt wrecked when our two mates got on the bike once more
And started off along the route that skirts around the shore,
But the beauty of that famous road was lost on poor old Jack,
Yet Tommy took the whole thing in, whilst sitting at the back!

'Look Jack, I see the Scottish coast,' he smiled, as they went on.
'That's wonderful,' puffed Jack, not looking up and feeling done!
'We're still not there! I'm punctured, Tommy, *seriously,* and you
Can stuff your face, stay cool and fresh and just admire the view!'

Now, once they got to Carnlough, Jack was ready to collapse.
'Why are you stoppin'?' Tommy asked. 'D'ye need to see the maps?'
'Tom, old mate,' Jack whispered, scarcely able to draw breath,
'Why aren't you knackered? Look at *me* – this ride's a livin' death!'

Eventually, against all odds, they entered their homerun
Through Waterfoot and Cushendall and on to Cushendun;
(In terms of speed, however, more like tortoise than like hare).
'Aw, finally.. Joe's,' Jack gasped. 'I thought we're never gettin' there!'

They set the tandem up Joe's path and knocked on his front door,

And sure, when Joe appeared, his jaw, it nearly hit the floor

To see our Jack and Tommy there, one fresh, the other wiped!

'Hey, how'd you lads get here?' he asked. Jack pointed to the bike..


And gasped, 'We came on that thing; think I must be off my head.

If I'd have gone another mile, son, I'd be tatey bread!'

With that, he staggered up the hall and crashed down on a seat;

'You lads must both be starving,' Kate said. 'Like a bit to eat?'


'I can't see how he's *room* for more,' said Jack. 'D'see your brother?

Made short work of an Ulster Fry, plus tea and toast, no bother;

What beats me, though, is how he's managed to arrive so bright

And here's me, half-dead, wonderin' how I'll make it back tonight!'


'Yes, that *is* curious', Kate said. 'Tommy, 'I'd not say you're fit

So, the difference between you two is strange, I must admit!

For, Tommy, Jack is really tired, and yet you're fine today;

Why aren't *you* stiff and sore like him, from pedalling all this way?'

'What *pedalling?*' asked Tommy. 'Sure, Kate, I was at the back!

Was I supposed to pedal, too? Was that not up to Jack?

I thought I'd just to hold on tight and let the wheels go roun'

And, once we'd built our speed up, let my legs just dangle down!'


Well! I thought you'd rather hear a quick commercial for our Coast

Than what Jack guldered! *'Do you know this route's among the most*

*Admired in all of Europe? – The tranquillity's a joy!'*

(Though I think *that* day they heard *Jack* in Glenariff and Glencloy!)


So, back to Jack and Tommy – yes, Kate fed them both real good,

But it neither calmed the atmosphere nor lightened up Jack's mood;

It didn't help that Joe and Kate were struggling not to laugh.

(It would have made a rare snap for the Belfast Telegraph!)


Well, eventually, the time came for the lads to take their leave

And, honestly, if you'd been there, you'd simply not believe

The sight of them, no words or smiles; then Tommy got a dunt

From Jack, to point him this time to the saddle at the *front!*

And then Jack broke his silence, 'Tommy, boy, it's up to you

To get us home in one piece; I don't mind just how you do!

I'm sittin' back, relaxin' and not gettin' one bit stressed –

No pedallin' for me, mate – I deserve a well-earned rest!'

# Dear Mr Claus...

## *a wishing tale...*

Now for a piece about Patrick, a nine-year old deep-thinking youngster who has featured in my poetry before! As always, his words mix a bit of boyish spirit with more serious matters in his mind. Here he is, just after his mum has suggested he writes a Christmas wish-list to send up the chimney to Santa.

Mum says that I must be respectful,

So I'm starting this, 'Dear Mr Claus,'

She also said, 'Don't be neglectful,'

Though I'm not too sure what that word does.


Well, I think it means that I should tell you

What I'd like for Christmas this year,

But first, do you think I might sell you

Some carrots for all your reindeer?


Mum tells us that she has to pay for

The presents that *we* get from you;

So, please bring some cash in your sleigh, for

Those carrots – and some shortbread, too –


And then Mum can send you our money

(That's if you can wait 'till next year);

I promise I'm not being funny –

You can use it for some Christmas cheer!

My mum says we're in a... *ree-session*

(I just might've spelt that word wrong);

I think that it means a depression,

So I'll try not to make this *too* long.


I like toys that are scientific,

Like robots and monsters, with names!

And, yes – please bring something terrific

This Christmas, for my brother, James!


My mum disapproves of toy weapons

But I say they're only for fun

So, with what my Aunt Clare calls *discretion*,

Do you think you could sneak me a gun?


Now, my *sister* will write you a letter

With a list seven times mine in length

But, to get all she asks down the chimney

Would take some incredible strength!

And besides, she is usually a bad girl,

In fact, she is bad all the time;

I think she's a bit of a sad girl,

And everyone calls her a slime!


I don't want to influence your judgement,

Mr Claus, but my brother and me

Might be feeling a bit of *begrudgement,*

If she finds all *she* wants by the tree!


Don't take this from me – do some checking

If she deserves one gift at all!

So, make sure your elf spies are tracking

The behaviour of Marie McCall!


Mr Claus, can I please tell you gently,

I think that this note-thing is slow

And, as not everyone has a chimney,

I'm not sure where *their* letters go.

Mr Claus, hope you don't mind me saying,

Writing lists is so way out-of-date;

Texts and emails are much less delaying

And those lists wouldn't get to you late!


So, I just hope that you won't be *too* mad

At this little suggestion from me –

Surely one of your elves has an i-pad

And can teach you a bit of I.T.


James says you are well past a hundred!

Today, online shopping's the craze;

If you got into that, I just wondered

Could Rudolph be put out to graze?


Yes! I'd like a space-hopper for bouncing,

And I've just one more big thing to add;

I don't suppose that you do counselling –

Could you get my mum back with my dad?

Naw, that isn't fair; I'll just leave things,

But I do have a wish now for you –

Please rest once you're through Christmas Eve. Things

Should be peaceful, 'till Boxing Day's through!

# Rapid Rabbit
# Restoration!

## *a neighbourly tale...*

This poem's based on a story someone told me many years ago and assured me was absolutely true! The names and location are my invention but, if you happen to know anything more about the actual story, I'd be fascinated to hear from you (and I'm sure the rabbit's owners would, too)!

In a suburb of Balbriggan, Shane and Mary McNamee

Lived in their spacious semi with a nice view of the sea;

Now, with daughter Bronagh wed,

Their Irish Terrier, Red

Made the number in the household up to three.


Now, while Shane and Mary waited for a grandchild to arrive,

Old Red the dog remained their focus, very much alive;

Active every single day,

Chasing cats and mice away,

His energy in constant overdrive.


Well, just across the garden fence lived Jim and Maureen Abbott,

A nice but fussy couple and their children, Jayne and Garrett;

Down their garden, in his hutch,

Was their family pet, called Sutch –

An expensive and much cherished lop-eared rabbit.


So, it happened that one sunny morning near the end of May,

The Abbotts took their children to the seaside town of Bray;

Shane and Mary were at home,

And though hills they loved to roam,

Thought they'd better do some gardening that day.

Well, Shane no sooner started weeding flowerbeds, when his eye
Just caught the sight of Red the dog, and something looked awry;
'Hey, Mary, what's Red shakin' –
Is it somethin' that he's taken?'
I think he's been on next door's side, but why?

Aw, saints preserve us, Mary – It's their rabbit in his mouth!
If Maureen gets a whiff of this, you'll hear her screams in Louth!
Both her and Jim hate Red
Since he dug up their rose bed,
So I think our friendship with them's just gone south!'

As Shane struggled to remove the rabbit from the jaws of Red,
To their horror, they could plainly see that poor old Sutch was dead!
'Shane, this is far from funny!
That rabbit cost them money,'
Gasped Mary. 'I don't *know* what can be said!

We daren't tell Jim and Mo the truth, yet we don't want to lie,'
She added. 'Shane, let's fix him up – a wash and a blow-dry!
If we clean up poor old Sutch,
Set him back inside his hutch,
It'll look as if his time just came to die..

For, Sutch is pretty old now – they'll just think he passed away
Quite peacefully, in comfort, sometime earlier today.'
'Yes, I agree,' said Shane,
'We should put him back again,
And they'll think he died when they went off to Bray!'

So, they set the rabbit on the floor inside their downstairs loo,
Then in came Mary with a basin and her best shampoo:
'Let's begin our big makeover,
He'll have fur as fresh as clover:
Brilliant – bouncy – bouffant – once we're through!'

So, they rubbed and scrubbed the rabbit for a long time in the basin
And inspected him to make sure there was not a single trace in
His fur of mud or gravel,
Or things that might unravel
Their denial of the truth. *(Such fabrication!)*

Well, washed and blow-dried, Sutch now looked a bunny once again!
'Right, Mary, I'll climb o'er the fence and put him in his pen,'
Said Shane. 'He's good as new,
So I'm thinkin' what I'll do
Is make sure everything's ten-out-of-ten..

Like, his door is lyin' open – how did old Red manage that?

And his water-bowl's turned over – what was our dog playin' at?

So, I'll fill the bowl up properly

And close the door, then hopefully

When they get back here, they won't smell a rat!'


Shane crossed the fence to Abbott's and he tidied up the hutch

Then, in the centre – pride of place – he carefully placed old Sutch;

His coat was white as snow,

Like the best pet in a show –

Their makeover had worked its magic touch!


So, back inside their kitchen, Shane and Mary felt relieved,

Although a little guilty that their neighbours they'd deceived;

'Right, let's have a cup of tea,'

Mary said. ''Tween you and me,

It *was* a clever plan that we conceived!'


'And necessary too,' said Shane, 'to save a lot of grief;

Imagine if the Abbotts knew that our Red was the thief

Who took and ate their pet,

Aw, there'd be no end, I'd bet

To what complaints we'd hear – beyond belief!'

'Well, anyhow,' said Mary, 'we have *spared* them that distress;
When they come back from Bray tonight, they'll go to bed, I guess;
But then, sometime tomorrow,
We'll hear about their sorrow
At Sutch's peaceful passing, nonetheless.'


So, Shane and Mary settled down (that had been one close call),
Content in both their minds that they had done what's best for all;
Then, just as it grew dark,
They heard the Abbotts park
Their car and lead the children up the hall.


Well, all was quiet. Shane and Mary sighed, 'They've gone to bed,'
When suddenly they heard a scream that would've roused the dead!
It was followed by some more,
'Till Shane looked out his door
At great commotion by Jim Abbott's shed.


Well, the Abbotts had gone crazy – Mo was shaking like a leaf,
Both their kids were screaming; Jim looked shocked beyond belief!
Shane asked, 'Are you okay?
Did things go wrong today –
An accident or run-in with a thief?'

Well, Jim and Mo could scarcely speak – they pointed to the hutch:
'Oh, Shane and Mary, something's happened – this is way too much!
The kids went out to stack
Their buckets at the back,
Then ran in panic, screaming, "Sutch! Sutch! Sutch!"'

Now Mary swallowed hard and asked them, 'Is old Sutch not well?'
Mo looked at her astonished: 'Sutch is dead – can you not tell?'
'Aw, we're sorry,' Shane replied,
'It's upsetting that he's died,
He looked all right – some things you can't foretell.

D'ye think he died this morning, after you'd gone off to Bray?'
'This morning?' Jim replied. 'He died *two weeks ago* today!
Sutch passed away in peace
And, once he was deceased,
We buried him just here. Did I not say?'

'How could this happen?' Mo exclaimed. 'We laid to rest old Sutch,
And we've come back this evening to him sitting in his hutch,
With his bowl filled to the brim,
Door on snib (folks, this is *grim*),
Without one trace of mud there – not a smutch!'

Then Jim asked, in bewilderment, 'Weren't *you* at home today?

Did things seem normal round our house the time we were away?'

'Oh, we didn't see a soul,'

Shane replied, 'but, on the whole,

Me and Mary were quite busy, anyway.'


At this, Mo grew hysterical: 'I have to beg your pardon,

But, didn't you say yesterday that you'd be in your garden?'

'Oh,' said Mary, with a smile,

'That was only for a while,

To water plants – you know how soil can harden.'


'I think I've known you long enough to tell that you're not lying,'

Said Jim. 'I need a whiskey,' while poor Mo, now beyond crying,

Asked Mary, 'Busy day?'

'*Argh,*' she thought, '*what can I say?*' –

'Oh, just a bit of... *cleaning...washing... drying!*'

# A Most Congenial Genie

## *a faraway tale...*

*Now for a truly surreal ballad. I suppose the moral of this story is: 'Be careful what you wish for!'*

Three Irish lads, a lot of years back – Kelly, Lynch and Doyle,

One from Wicklow, one from Galway, one from outside Boyle,

Signed up to go to sea

On the good ship Rosalie,

As it set out one fine morning from the Foyle.


They scarcely knew each other, but they'd joined to see the world,

And watched in fascination as the mainsail was unfurled,

Their excitement not surprisin'

As they sailed to the horizon,

Whilst around them, mighty waves both crashed and swirled!


So, with the captain and the crew, they crossed great oceans three;

Lynch charted maps and Kelly steered while Doyle, he made the tea.

But then, a great storm roared,

And our lads fell overboard,

And were washed up on an isle in some far sea.

The lads came round and saw that they were on a sandy shore,

With rocks and inlets all around and palm trees by the score;

The island was quite small;

Lynch said, 'We'll explore it all,

But it's best we form an action plan before.'


'So, we should all spread out and search for food,' young Kelly said,

'I see some mangoes turning ripe, just there beside a glade.'

'And I'll fetch some coconuts,'

Said Lynch, without a fuss.

Said Doyle, 'I'll dig for *spuds*, if there's a spade!'


Sure, Lynch, he was the brainy one, and Kelly was quite practical,

But Doyle? Well, let's suffice to say he wasn't that pragmatical;

Next, Lynch drew up a sketch,

Then Kelly went to fetch

Some wood to build a hut – quite understandable.

Then Lynch said, 'We'll need bait for fishing; I've just found a grub,'

Whilst Kelly rubbed two sticks together, lighting twigs and scrub;

Said Doyle, 'I'll wander round,

And I'd better bring a pound

In the off-chance that there just might be a pub!'


Well, that was how it started, and things went from bad to worse

And, after *five long years* marooned, they scarcely could converse

As, though this sounds rather sad,

Doyle just drove the others mad –

'That man,' said Lynch, 'has brought some sort of curse!'


'Do you recall,' said Kelly, 'we asked Doyle to build a boat?

He spent three long years buildin' it to find it wouldn't float,

For he chose wood from a tree

That was clearly *ebony*,

Yet it kept him out of *our* way, stupid goat!'

Then *ten years passed.* Each day, Lynch put a mark upon a tree;

(By this stage, each lad had a beard that reached down to his knee).

No ship ever sailed that way,

Though they watched out every day,

Then one morning 'twas Doyle's turn to scan the sea.


Now, after he'd been on the beach awhile, he thought he'd nap,

'Sure no ships ever sail near here – we must be off the map!'

But he scarcely had reclined

When he spied the strangest find –

What seemed like buried treasure – rare, not scrap!


He scratched his head and wondered what this artefact might be:

'I'd better take it back and let the other fellas see

What kind o' thing I've found,

That's been buried in the ground;

Why, it looks like some old pot for makin' tea!'

He took it back to camp. The others asked, 'What did ye bring?'

Said Doyle, 'When I was on the beach, I found this strange old thing;

Can ye work out what it is?'

Lynch said, 'My analysis?

Some type of lamp – looks golden, like a ring..


Let's clean it up a bit, I'm fairly *sure* it's made of gold;

It might've been left here by some great eastern ship of old!'

Then Kelly, thereupon

Rubbed the lamp until it shone,

And, *'WHOOSH!'* a mighty sight they did behold!


For, suddenly, before their eyes, a *genie* darted out,

Accompanied by sparks and smoke from deep inside the spout!

Well, the lads, amidst the din,

Nearly jumped out of their skin,

Scared witless by what *now* had come about!

'I am the genie of the lamp,' the mystic figure said,

'And any wish I can make true; of me you might have read.

I can grant you only *three*,

So you must choose carefully;

You each have *one*– whatever's in your head!'


Well, Lynch was first to go: 'I've been marooned with these two men

For countless years and, Genie, it's been driving me insane!

Oh, to smell the peat once more,

At my home on Galway's shore –

I wish that I was back in dear old Ireland once again!'


And so, *'VAMOOSH!'* away he went!  His wish was not in vain!

Then Kelly said, 'Yeah, stuck here with these lads was one big pain;

I'd love to be at home,

Oh, those Wicklow hills to roam –

I wish that I was back in dear old Ireland once again!'

And so it came to Doyle's turn: 'Well, I've not got Lynch's brain

Or Kelly's hands to get by on this island, it is plain;

And, with Lynch and Kelly gone,

I'll be lonely on my own –

I wish that Lynch and Kelly were back here with me again!'

# Dymphna Delaney

## *a tale of changing fortune...*

*We love it when we think everything's going well – but do we ever grow too confident? Here's the light-hearted story of someone who seemed to get sucked into that trap. Imagine you're one of Dymphna's friends who has just spotted her sitting alone in her local pub.*

Hi - how are you doin'?

I feel like a ruin

Tonight. Will you look at me, now?

Well, what d'ye think –

Here's me havin' a drink

By myself.  Ach, ye'll want a pow-wow!


Me? – Dymphna Delaney:

Gregarious? Zany?

Well, this evenin', I'm feeling, ach…down;

I know you'll expect

A fair bit o' craic,

An' tonight here's me wearin' a frown!


Your askin' me why?

Ach, sit down and I'll try

To explain to you what's goin' wrong;

I'll just have to say,

It's been awful today!

Well, folks, without makin' a song..

And dance of it... So,

Four Tuesdays ago,

I was walkin' home from Fahey's Shop

When, suddenly, I,

With the tail of my eye,

Saw something that caused me to stop.


It was only two Euro,

But I'd to be sure, though

Of what lay there glintin' at me;

Then, as I stooped down,

Growin' there, on the ground,

Was a rare *four-leaf clover* – *YIPPEE!*


It's my firm belief

That this sort of leaf

Brings fortune to woman or man –

So, without much ado,

I reached where it grew

And, to tell you the truth, nearly ran..

Home that mornin'

And already was formin'

A plan, should it bring me good luck;

At the same time, I got

An empty flower pot

And filled it with soil, manure, muck..


To plant this rare clover,

And then set it over

Beside my back wall, on a dish

Sayin', 'Girl, what a find!'

Then made up my mind –

Each Tuesday, I'd make me a wish!


Then the followin' week,

My boss, Hugh McPeake,

Said I'd got a rise in my pay;

Well, I nearly *hugged* Hugh –

The wish had come true

That I'd made that *second Tues-day!*

Well, I sure liked that rise

And though 'penny wise

And pound foolish' had long been my motto,

*Next Tuesday* I went –

First time ever – and spent

A bit o' my cash on the Lotto!


I'd just done it for fun

But, guess what? I won,

And landed myself sixteen million!

I think I fell over

And gasped, 'It's that clover!

I'll go out and rent a pavilion..


To have a soiree,

To celebrate me

And my fortune, the following week!'

So I chose *Tuesday* night,

To ensure things went right,

With a dress code expensive and chic!

Well, I wished for romance

And, there, just by chance,

Was a friend of my cousin, James Faye;

His name's Pete O'Keefe

And it stretches belief –

Yet another *amazing Tues-day!*


For, I'm *datin'* this fella

From outside Killala

And, wait 'till you hear what he does –

He's Director of Sales

For all Ireland and Wales,

In a software firm called Price and Maws!


And, if that's not enough,

(And this is no bluff),

He has a boat anchored in Crete;

We're goin' this Spring,

And there might be a ring,

If I play the old cards right with Pete!

Yet, here's me tonight,

Doubtless lookin' a sight

And feelin' a bit out-of-tune;

Are you wonderin' why

I've a tear in my eye?

I guess you'll be knowin' quite soon.


D'ye need me to say?

It's *Tuesday* today,

Near midnight – there goes the last shout!

There's been *nothin'* this week,

The outlook's so bleak –

*Could it be that my luck's just run out?*

# Murder? - It's a Case of 'Man's Laughter'

## *a tale of two jokers...*

*I like a play on words, and this ballad has two of them. The first one's in the title: 'manslaughter' = 'man's laughter'! Now I'll not tell you the second one, as you'll find out at the end!*

A couple of construction workers, both from Tullamore,
Ed Flynn and Terry Brown, could tell conundrums by the score
And, as for jokes and rigmaroles, the two were never stuck,
Should they be in the pub or digging in four feet of muck!

Now, a certain day in Offaly, the two were hard at work,
Laying drainage pipes across a field near Cloneyhurke;
Then, just before their lunch break finished, Terry turned to Ed:
 'Hey, have you any new jokes, boy, inside that daft old head?'

Ed scratched that head a moment, then he said, 'I might have one
You haven't heard; here's how it goes: "This farmer met a nun..."'
And so the tale went on – there was a leprechaun, a goldmine,
A giant and fifteen pints of stout before it reached its punch line!

Well, Terry started laughing and he simply couldn't stop!
'Ah, come on, man,' responded Ed, 'this is *way* o'er the top!'
But Terry only laughed the louder, such was his compulsion
And staggered left and right, like he was having a convulsion!

Now, Ed just watched, incredulous, as Terry doubled sore
And tried to catch his breath before he'd start to laugh some more!
'Hey, careful!  Watch out!' guldered Ed. 'Just look behind you! Yipes!'
As Terry tumbled down the ditch beside the drainage pipes.

'Ye great big eejit!' shouted Ed. 'Now look at what ye've done!'
And wondered if his mate had just rolled down the bank for fun.
'Ach, come on, boy! Get on yer feet !' he growled at him, until
He noticed that his old pal lay there slumped and very still.

'Hey, Terry, are ye all right, mate?' asked Ed, 'What did you do?'
'D'ye know your sittin' in a sewer? Does that not bother you?'
Then, worried, he exclaimed the first thing that came in his head:
'Hey, I don't want to scare you, mate – d'ye think ye might be dead?'

Just then, the foreman of the work, a man called Albert Strong
Decided he'd walk over to see what was going on;
At first he said, 'This fellow's sleepin', think I'll dock his pay!'
Said Ed, 'I don't think he'll be doin' any more today!'

'What happened: did ye push him?' Albert asked, with anxious frown.
'I only told a joke,' said Ed. 'He laughed, then just fell down!'
'You mean this man *died laughing*? You expect me to believe this?'
Said Albert. 'Get the ambulance and police, we can't just leave this!'

So, round came Sergeant Foley, armed with notebook and a pen,
Who first surveyed the scene, then asked the boss about the men:
'Were these two workers decent lads, or was one a wrongdoer,
Who'd kill the other in cold blood and leave him in a sewer?'

'You'd better ask the man himself,' said Albert, calling Ed.
'You're Mr Flynn, sir?' Foley asked. 'Your boss says this man's dead
And you're the only witness to what happened; tell me more.'
'I told a joke, he started laughin', then he hit the floor!'

The sergeant rolled his eyes and asked, 'Was there a reason why
You planned to make him laugh so hard you knew he'd likely die?
If so, what was your motive? Did you owe him any money?'
'No, sir,' said Ed, 'I didn't think the joke was all *that* funny!

Besides sir, if you're lookin' for a motive, let me say,
He *asked* me if I knew a joke that he'd not heard today.
I simply told the first one I remembered – that is plain,
And didn't know that it would leave him lifeless in a drain!'

'That changes things,' the sergeant said. '*He* asked a joke of *you*,
Regardless of the fact that you're a joker, through-and-through,
And laughed so hard, he slumped against a drainage-pipe and died?
I think I can conclude: this is a case of – *sewer-side!*'

# The Ballad of Brendan Bambrick's Beard!

## *a tale of misinterpretation...*

*We've had the barely believable and the seriously surreal, but now to the REALLY ridiculous! It's just a nonsense poem I quickly made up and thought I'd include it in this collection!*

I've the longest beard in Ireland!

Here's me standin' in Ardee,

It stretches through Kilkenny,

And it ends up in Tralee;

That's once it circles Mullingar

And zigzags through Kildare,

Traverses Tipperary

And meanders round Rosslare!


Now, I'll bet you all are askin',

'Well, how *did* it grow so long?'

Believe me, I'm not jokin' –

It would stretch from Bray to Cong!

I shave it off each mornin'

But, by evenin', it's grown back!

Sometimes it's grey or ginger

And, at other times, it's black!

I'm sure you won't believe me
But, me good mates Dec and Sean
An' me were walkin' from the pub
An' saw this leprechaun!
He said, 'Good evenin', fellas!
By this week, I've got to reach
Me quota of three wishes, so
Why don't you have one each?'

'Well now,' thought Dec, 'I'm kind o' tired,'
So he spoke first and said,
'I need a good sleep every night –
I'd like a nice new bed!'
Sean thought, 'I'm kind o' hungry,'
And said, 'If you are able,
I'd like that each night I come home,
There's plenty on the table!'

Now, when it came to my turn,

I found it hard to think

Of what I really wanted,

(Well, I'd had a bit to drink);

I thought, 'I'm kind o' thirsty,'

But I think he didn't hear –

'Each night,' I said, 'the thing I'd like

Is Ireland's longest...*BEER!*'

# Harry Ward: The Wake

## *a spontaneous tale...*

*Sometimes there's a very narrow line between the sad and the humorous, as illustrated in this poem! Although Harry is a fictional character, this rather fitting incident at his wake would certainly have amused him – and made him even more legendary!*

Near the town of Ennistymon lived a man called Harry Ward,

And just about the whole of Munster this old man adored

For his stories, wit and blether

And, no matter what the weather,

If you'd met him, you would laugh with one accord!


But it wasn't just the blarney that attracted folk to Harry,

It was his wealth of wisdom that persuaded them to tarry,

Just to hear each anecdote

And, give him a song's first note

And the melody of most he'd clearly carry!


I think old Harry sang in every pub in County Clare,

From Kilrush to Lisdoonvarna – sure, you'd find him sitting there,

With his glass of stout in hand,

And, not needing any band,

Why, he'd sing his heart and soul out anywhere!

Now I think old Harry had a heart of thirty carat gold,

Sure, generous to a fault he was, alike to young and old;

Yes, a truly decent lad,

And you'd never hear a bad

Word from his mouth; he'd neither grump nor scold.


Then sadly, one cold winter's night, old Harry passed away;

His nephews, Ray and Ciaran, journeyed over from Roscrea.

Soon the news spread near and far,

'Till it seemed like every car

On the island rolled up for his wake next day!


When the undertaker pulled up, Ray and Ciaran looked around,

For not a place to set old Harry's coffin could be found.

Said Ciaran, 'Grab some chairs

From the spare room up the stairs,

But you'd better raise your voice above the sound..

Of talkin' – it's important that they all hear what you say.'

'Folk, can we have three chairs for Harry?' thundered nephew Ray;

For a second, all went quiet,

Then erupted like a riot –

As, in unison, they roared: 'Hip! Hip! Hooray!'

# 10, 9, 8, 7... Lift-Off at Cape Innishannon!

## *a space-age tale...*

*I actually saw a church tower like this, towering above the trees, which locals and passers-by likened to a space rocket. It was too good an opportunity to miss!*

In a quiet little town in Ireland stands Saint Patrick's Church,

Surrounded by a host of trees – horse chestnut, oak and birch;

Well, towering high above those trees, folk say, as they arrive,

The steeple looks at first glance like the rocket 'Saturn V'.


Now, Russell P. Zokowski from the State of Tennessee

Was on a visit, tracking down his genealogy

And, driving his convertible, he stopped for some reflection

As, slightly lost, he thought it best to stop and ask direction.


Now, Sean and Pat, two local lads, just happened to be there

As Russell pulled up and, in no time, this congenial pair

Explained to him which way to go, then suddenly his eye

Caught sight of that same tall church steeple pointing to the sky!


'Hey, see *that* thing,' he asked them, 'towering high above the trees?

It's like a rocket on a launch-pad!  What's this? Tell me, please!'

Sean winked at Pat, then turned and, with a perfectly straight face

Said, 'Have ye not heard Ireland's sendin' lads up into space?

We're trainin' astronauts right now in my dad's old cowshed,

And flight control base is a tower two miles from Malin Head;

The launch-pad is the best there is, a long time in the plannin',

The same as your Cape Kennedy. This Is… Cape Innishannon!'


'So, Ireland's joined the space-race?' Russell asked, incredulous.

'Then, why have I not heard about this? Why no great big fuss?

Hey, maybe you're just kidding me – I'm guessing very soon

You'll laugh that I thought Ireland's sending men up to the moon!'


'The moon's already done!' smiled Sean. 'Our mission's bigger still!'

'That's right,' grinned Pat, 'the scale of it just gives us such a thrill,'

Then said, with staid expression masking his great sense of fun,

'The astronauts we're sendin' will be landin' on the *sun!*'


'Now, hang on, boys,' said Russell, 'that ol' sun is mighty hot!

You're setting out to land on it? – You'll sure end in a lot

Of trouble there! Now, please don't think I'm out to scare you, right,

But its temperature is well above *two-thousand Farenheit..*

So, boys, your craft will need to be impregnable and slick,
With shield of carbon-composite, let's say, five inches thick,
To tolerate that awful heat, the solar winds, eruptions –
I'll bet the cost to Ireland's budget causes lots of ructions!'

'All that sounds too expensive,' Pat replied. 'But you should know,
A lad from Ireland's Space Department came here days ago
With bits of aluminium like they're usin' on the flight,
Askin, "Have you got a heater or a furnace we can light..

To test this thing's resistance?" Well, the hottest thing we knew
Was my Auntie Mary's oven, so for, say, an hour or two
We stuck it in and turned it high; it worked without a doubt,
For she'd to wrap a tea-towel round it, just to lift it out!

So, our astronauts are good to go – the checks have all been done
On Ireland's first space mission, sendin' fellas to the sun;
And, with respect, we won't need carbon-something ten foot thick –
Our scientists in Ireland haven't missed the obvious trick!

And, you big nations in the space-race? Just you sit and scoff –

Our astronauts know what they're doin', they're not blastin' off

In the middle o' the daytime, when the sun is shinin' bright –

We've got the whole thing figured out – they're goin' up at night!'

# Glossary:

**Balbriggan:** *a town on the east coast of Ireland, north of Dublin.*

**Begrudgement:** *there's debate over whether this word really exists, but I did see it on an official paper and, besides, Patrick's use of it only adds to its authenticity!*

**Blarney:** *nonsensical, humorous talk, sometimes used to charm the listeners. Kissing the 'Blarney Stone' on the battlements of Blarney Castle in County Cork is said to endow that person with 'the gift of the gab' (eloquence in speech).*

**Blether:** *to talk a lot of nonsense, particularly in a long-winded way.*

**Brave wee bit away:** *quite a distance.*

**Bray:** *a seaside town / resort in County Wicklow, south of Dublin.*

**Buckna:** *a place near Ballymena in County Antrim.*

**Castlereagh:** *a district in east Belfast.*

**Craic:** *either news ('What's the craic?') or a bit of fun ('Think of the craic!')*

**Cushendun:** *a coastal village in County Antrim.*

**Cut o' them:** *the look of them (implying that it is comical).*

**Dour:** *gloomy.*

**Dunt:** *an impatient nudge, a 'dig' with an elbow.*

**Fair bob:** *a reasonable amount of money.*

**Footer:** *work at something without really knowing what you're doing.*

**Gawky:** *a bit ungainly / awkward.*

**Good man yer da:** *a Belfast way of expressing a compliment or saying 'Well done!'*

**Innishannon:** *a village in County Cork, chosen at random as the site of the imaginary Irish space project.*

**Lurgan spade:** *looking miserable – having a 'long face'.*

**Malin Head:** *the northernmost point in Ireland, in County Donegal – it just makes Pat and Sean's story more absurd!*

**Man dear:** *a sigh, or expression of incredulity.*

**Puttin' on a bit:** *putting on weight.*

**Quare oul geg:** *a very good laugh; good fun.*

**Real McCoy:** *genuine – the real thing.*

**Sinch:** *'It will be easy'.*

**Startin' to blow:** *beginning to boast.*

**Tatey bread:** *rhyming slang – dead.*

**Ulster Fry:** *something like a full English breakfast, but served with soda and potato bread (two local specialities).*

**Wake:** *the traditional Irish wake is well documented. As Harry's wake is set in more recent times, the form it takes is the modern 'toned-down' version but in this case it's still a rather noisy affair.*

**Year o' dot:** *as long as anyone can remember.*

**Z'at a mask?** *'Is that a mask?'*